# PRAISE FOR *ROCK STARS*

"*Rock Stars* by Matt Mason is a book of poetry with a fierce beat, a book you can dance to! Mason's poems invoke Blondie, the Go-Go's, Prince, Poison, Bon Jovi, Duran Duran, Flock of Seagulls, Blue Oyster Cult, Lionel Richie, David Bowie—just to name a few. (Truly! There's more...) As nostalgic as the surface noise of a needle hitting a vinyl record, these poems will transport you back to the 80's. But lest you think Mason is stuck in the past, his stunning poems are also road maps for the young. In fact, who but Matt Mason, can write a poem "Graduation Address to the Kinder Kingdom Awesome Tots Preschool Class of 2023"? This book is delightful in every way!"

—DENISE DUHAMEL, AUTHOR OF *SECOND STORY*

"Matt Mason's poems have energy. Matt Mason's poems have drive, and craft, and heart, and excitement, and funny lines like "I want to see two words rhyme / who never thought of each other that way be-fore"—lines which harken back to other things Mason's poems have, such as tenderness and wildness and celebrations of young and other kinds of love—love of music, family, laughter, and good poems, which, by the way, Matt Mason's *Rock Stars* is full of."

—CHARLES HARPER WEBB,
AUTHOR OF *SIDEBEND WORLD* AND *URSULA LAKE*

"Imagine being introduced to the musicians responsible for the soundtrack of the 1980s, along with the poets of the 1820s and 1930s. Then imagine being invited with them on a long car ride through your favorite concerts, your fiery consciences, and to your final concerns. Matt Mason is at the wheel and this book is a mixtape—an ode and ovation to what our ears taught us before we knew what to say. Back then, we made these tapes not just to capture the sound, but as an attempt at an emotional mnemic, to capture a very specific feeling of time and to pass that time on to those we love. The people and the

T0000147

sounds eulogized herein aren't necessarily gone, but their mentorship—that which is very somewhat responsible for the beat-nik-boxing of Matt's heart—deserves no better epitaph than the one you are about to spin. Matt clearly loves us."

—MIGHTY MIKE MCGEE,
SANTA CLARA COUNTY POET LAUREATE EMERITUS, 2018–2019

"Matt Mason's *Rock Stars* lifts joyful noise across the austerity as it vacillates between nostalgia for the 80s and the demands of the present. There's wry humor in the poems, as they convene with canonical poets, stay true to hair bands, new wave bands, alt-rock bands, and as they elevate toward homilies. *Rock Stars* is rich with allusions which delight like little Easter Eggs. It's an abundant and dazzling paean to the songs and souls that fascinate us."

—MICHAEL KLEBER-DIGGS, AUTHOR OF *WORLDLY THINGS*

# ROCK STARS

# ROCK STARS

Poems by
### Matt Mason

Button Publishing Inc.
Minneapolis
2023

ROCK STARS

POETRY

AUTHOR: Matt Mason

COVER DESIGN: Amy Law

AUTHOR PHOTO: Cindy Grady

❖

ALL RIGHTS RESERVED

© 2023 by Matt Mason

❖

# butt⦿n p⦿etry

Published by Button Poetry

Minneapolis, MN 55418 | http://www.buttonpoetry.com

❖

Manufactured in the United States of America

PRINT ISBN: 978-1-63834-065-2

EBOOK ISBN: 978-1-63834-066-9

AUDIOBOOK ISBN: 978-1-63834-070-6

First printing

For the artists who've influenced, inspired,
entertained, and pushed me.


With thanks to the Kimmel Harding Nelson Center in Nebraska City
for the time and space to get parts of this manuscript collected.
And, especially, to Sarah.

# CONTENTS

# SIDE 1

# TRACK 1

# RAPTURE


is the best song by Blondie.
It makes you feel
like there's no other choice
but to raise your arms up
and shake your feet.
Even the
man from Mars eating cars disco rap weird bits,
all of it.
Debbie Harry's voice swoons to a command,
the piper playing to the wicker basket of cobras and
inhibitions be damned.

Though,
when you hear it in a Chipotle
in your forties, seated
across from your nine-year-old daughter,

you realize
there are
limitations

to enchantments, to how much you
can get away with
shaking; that,

once,
you could let it all go,
and who would care,
could carpe all the damn diem you dare, and
in this chain-burrito experience,
in this age of greying hair, this
rapture
where, while gravity
holds you tight to your chair,

all around you

others

are lifted

one by one

into the air.

# TRACK 2

## SHOULD IT MAKE A DIFFERENCE ON MY APPLICATION

I do have a lot of poems
about eighties rock.

This is based off
my ten-year residency

being alive
in the eighties

and driving
a Ford Escort with a tape deck.

I've also known other
poets, like David Blair, who

have amazing eighties rock poems.

Blair's was about Journey.
"Don't Stop Believin'."

I have a poem about Blair's poem about Journey.
So there's that.

I specialized in Dire Straits
though am versed

in the works of
Bon Jovi, Blondie, and more, with

branches to earlier influences going back
to Zeppelin, Bowie, and early Bee Gees. So

when do I start?

## ASH WEDNESDAY, WORKING AT THE GROUP HOME

A gentle client sits
watching Cathedral Mass on TV,
sound turned all the way down,
while her radio on top of it shakes with a revival of eighties rock,

and
in a shot
it makes sense, it
makes sense

you want to be
inside this church,
Go-Go's singing like the Spirit
so different from the one you came of age in,

this bubble
with a choir
lifting joyful noise
across the austerity,

ancient priest
smudging pink-sweatered ladies' foreheads
while angels
howl, *We got the beat!*

No monotone chant to "rise,"
it's, *Everybody get on your feet*;
maybe you'd all have still rebelled,
maybe you'd still be a prodigal,

maybe our generation
wouldn't have given a damn about Michael Stipe,
but, at some point,
we'd all have come back

to our knees,
saying,
hand me my sackcloth,
hand me my ash,

it's time
to dance.

## WHEN WE SAW PRINCE

Our daughter was inside a belly stretched five-months
taut, we weren't scared of
decibels, we were counting on them, filled with
hopes of what one will absorb in utero.

No, she hasn't spontaneously taken to
purple raiments, her piano lessons have not gone
nova in a chromosomally unexplainable funkiness, but

we have certitude that one does not backstroke in the amnion's
        current to
such strobe, such electricity, while the body and brain are finding
their ways and not be touched; this gestation

takes patience: we feed her bones to strength,
illuminate her in art museums,
soak her in poetry, we humbly expect nothing

but transcendence.

TRACK 3

## ON KANSAS 156

All the radio has to say
is eighties rock

and Kenny Rogers.
You get behind

a horse trailer
and stay there

because you can't see
around it, and,

oh man,
the radio seek stops

on "Right Down the Line,"
Gerry Rafferty making love sound uncrappy

whether you're ten
with a fresh copy of *City to City* in your hands

or forty-five with your two daughters
bored in the backseat;

you feel helpless
as the station starts to slip

into static, last lines
of the song in and out,

oil pumps and grain towers,
cassettes you forgot

how they broke
after too many plays,

unspooling
deep

inside
your bones.

## US-54

Passing through Hooker, Oklahoma,
radio's all God and mariachi,

slow drawl and passionate croon,
*howdy, howdy, howdy,* and *mi corazón*

up and down the dial. By Texhoma,
Glen Campbell injects pedal steel and fiddle,

tumbleweeds of culture blow
radio tower to radio tower

in dust and static
down the highway.

## CALLED BY CHRIST


Phone rings.
I pick up.
He says,
*AM Country Radio!*
Hangs up.

All afternoon
I listen in my car like a
kid again, kneeling at the altar in a white shirt, waiting
for the taste of First Communion,
station to station
as if eternal life comes down to this.

Every one
is fiddle
and twang
and wrong.

I get paranoid,
get angry,
hearing voices
all the way from Chicago and Topeka, crackles
of a traffic report from Texas,
dozens saying
nothing,

punctuated with Paul Harvey at different verses in a page
about the tragic deaths
of three soldiers in Iraq and this amazing Bose radio.
No secret knowledge,
no higher message
here.

And then AM 640 out of Tulsa
buzzes, *And have You*
*been called*
*by Jesus,*

my eyes bloom in the rearview,
*out of sin?*
What's left to answer but, *I don't know,*
*I think I've been called to too many ballads about lovin' mah country*
        *and the women who love too much, not enough, and not at*
        *all!*

AM 640 maybe rebuts that
but it rolls in gulps
of static,
and I feel real superior
and then feel stupid
and lost.

      Day 2

He calls back.
It's nothing dramatic,
no midnight, 3 a.m.
He only says, *How*
*is that poetry?*
*Reads like toaster directions.*

*And leave Paul Harvey out of it.*
*He understands the sound*
*of baking bread.*
Click.

      Day 3

Phone rings.
I panic
because now Paul Harvey
is in the poem twice.

Make that three times.
I answer on the fourth ring.
It's only Aaron
from Credit Card Services; he has exciting great news about

Day 4

Jesus tells me Aaron really could have saved me
some money, and that if I could fit a sunrise
into muffin tins, it
would redefine almost all the top-tier adjectives.

When I don't say anything,
Jesus asks if I imagine colors
as I speak someone's name,
goes on how my wife's
is pink-tinged green
in such a way that magnolias, especially,
admire.

When I don't say anything,
He coughs a little,
says He's really gotta run,
says He's got a lot to do today,
and take care,
and click.
And dial tone.

When I hit last-call return,
I just get a donut shop downtown.

And that doesn't sound nearly as good tonight
as it should.

# TRACK 4

## SAMUEL TAYLOR COLERIDGE AND ACCEPTANCE OF PERSONAL IMMATURITY

*"Every rose has its thorn*
*just like every night has its dawn*
*just like every cowboy sings a sad, sad song,*
*every rose has its thorn."*
—Poison


You still cry
when you hear that song on the radio.

And you know
if anyone knew this,
they'd call you a baby.

Even the babies.
Even your mother.
When a girl dumped Coleridge

like a janitor dumps a bucket of warm grey water,
like she dumped you,

he cried too.
Then he made up
a new life:

no more of this
namby pamby "Sam Coleridge," he would change
his name to Silas Tomkyn Comberbache; no

puny student, he,
adventurer now, freedom fighter, soldier in the light dragoons!

Until bored. And aching. He realized this to be
neither adventurous nor
in any way free.

When he unraveled
back to Oxford, Sam
laughed loud

with the lions, gathered round fresh kills of beer and sausage
but kept a steel jaw hammered to his face,

a face buried, it would seem,
deep inside his books
every time the singers,

with their hair and pants gone feral,
break
from heavy madrigal thunder

into the slow,
sad
ballad.

## JOHN KEATS

John Keats burned
for sex and death,
got the one too late,
the other, well, yes,
and left us
with holes
in our manuscripts,
all of us,
hands rifling our ribcages
like pockets, searching
for what we know isn't there

but pray our fingers will chime up against
anyway.

## SHELLEY

The body washed ashore, face
scoured like blue glass,
every edge rounded, masquerading
as a pebble. But they recognized
him as Percy Bysshe Shelley by the book
still buttoned in a jacket pocket.
This cold face, this soft stranger
identified
by John Keats' testimony
held against his heart,
hearing each
last beat
until
you could
not tell it
anymore
from the tide.

## WILLIAM BLAKE'S WINDOW

*"The birds are in their trees,*
*the toast is in the toaster,*
*and the poets are at their windows."*
—From "The Trouble with Poetry" by Billy Collins


*"[Blake] himself recalls a childhood episode in which*
*he saw God pressing his face against a windowpane."*
—From *The English Romantics* by John L. Mahoney


You saw God's breath frost your windowpanes, William, you
intimate of miracle and blasphemy, writing
so wildly your words turn
untamed, snarl across anthologies
at sycophants and confessionals, claw
at pages where only lion tamers
like Shelley or Coleridge dare
share your chapters; O, William,
burning bright,
we hold up
lighters for you,
call for encores, call
in quiet nights
where we sit tired
of the little gospels
we script to crisp and tidy papers,
our windows filled
only with moonlight,
dark fields.

# TRACK 5

## IT'S NOT THE COP'S FAULT


It's not the cop's fault
the cruiser video cam clicks on
as soon as his flashers do, so
in court we see
he was rockin' out
to Bryan Adams singin'
"Straight from the Heart."

Oh, Officer Soft Jams,
parked on the median
of the thoroughfare of my heart,
I can't deny I was following too close,
but I will not sign your consent to search form;
if you really want me to open up,
you're going to need a warrant.

## IT IS 1997, KARAOKE BAR, DES MOINES,


Tonight's the night you choose to fistfight Tom Jones.
You write his name on the piece of paper above
"It's Not Unusual," hand it
to the DJ, KJ, whatever the word is,
and you sit,
you deal with the "Whip It" of it,
you deal with the sight of Rick Astley
delivered in unironic flaunt,
you deal with "You Give Love a Bad Name" partially crooned,
partially screeched
like some Bon Jovi centaur has crashed through the room,

before they announce your name
(which you have not aliased
(which could be a mistake,
you hope-filled son or daughter of hope-filled parents
(you were somebody's dream))).

You give new truth
to lines like,
*It's not unusual*
*to see me cry.*
*I want*
*to die.*

And it is glorious.
Even better than your "How Deep Is Your Love"
(spoiler alert: not very)
that you gave as a gift
to a different karaoke bar last week.

Someone
takes an obligatory ride in "Little Red Corvette,"
someone human centipedes a different Bon Jovi beast together,
someone disregards human decency and sings "We Built This City on
        Rock and Roll,"

then
one of the regulars
dressed in a style
you can't quite put a name to
saunters up with attitude,
stands in that spotlight
like it is their main source of nourishment,
stares you down
as he takes that song back,
he Not Unusuals the crap out of it,
like some alternate incarnation of Mike Tyson,
he bites the second verse's goddamn ear off, he—

oh, "Gilligan Chic,"
that's the name
for how he's dressed—he

takes this serious,
he's there to lay hands on this song like Jesus Karaoke Christ,
as if Tom Jones once saved him from drowning
or wolves
or being shipwrecked on some uncharted desert isle.

*Bully to you, my good man,*
you want to say,
*you have bested me
in something almost as ridiculous
as competition poetry;*

*now sit your white-pants ass down,
the DJ, KJ, VJ, BJ hasn't even gotten to my slip for "Delilah"
or "She's a Lady,"*

*buckle up,
son,
this
was only ever
Round
One.*

# MONTAGE!

It's raining. Bus stop. Four plastic grocery bags
looped on one wrist. Time
is not moving. Some great Pause button
on the universal VHS player
has been pushed. Headlights hang
above the road like lanterns. You just missed
that last bus and wish
it could all speed up, that some music
would kick up a glam boot and pretend to rock
for some band made entirely of hairspray and tattoo ink
sweating to exhort you to an epic against-the-odds victoriousness as
       the next hour passes in a quick series of clips set to the beat.

The clips
would kind of suck.
Flash: you
wiping drizzle off your forehead, Flash:
you checking the time on a phone whose battery's close to done,
       Flash:
you wiping a layer of wet off the bus bench, Flash:
pensive shot of you thinking about sitting, Flash:
you not sitting.

It ain't *Rocky IV*
where they knew
how to montage;

by then, the eighties were halfway spent,
the montage was being perfected, and, bam,
*Rocky IV* took it down and nailed its head to the wall, raised all
       stakes;
three-quarters of the movie
was fast-motion thumping reminiscent of "Eye of the Tiger"
but not as memorable,
a montage of montages as they up-montaged the art of montage to
       maximum montage magnitude.

This ain't that.
This ain't "Eye of the Tiger."
It's more "You're the Best" by Joe Esposito,
a song that was supposed to be over the *Rocky III* montage
that "Eye of the Tiger" ended up soundtracking,
was supposed to make a montage
in *Flashdance* until "Maniac" knocked it off the cassette
and it waxed on to *Karate Kid*, though
nobody remembers it was there.

A red Kia just splashed a puddle halfway up your thighs.

You
are ready to fast forward,
head nodding,
foot tapping,
trying to push
this shit
to get real.

# TRACK 6

## TED KOOSER

Ted Kooser, former US Poet Laureate,
would wake up at 4
to write
before going to his insurance job.
It's 4:49.
I have been watching
this piece of paper for
a while now.
Ted won a Pulitzer. I
have thought about words
like "possum,"
"sarcophagus,"
"Gorbachev,"
none of which have done more
than curl up
and cough. The world,
so dark and hushed,
hangs above our heads,
waiting to break
like cold eggs, the sky
black as cast iron. Ted
will go to work soon. I
am waiting
to start.

## NOTES WRITTEN AFTER ROBERT BLY'S
## "LOOKING AT A DEAD WREN IN MY HAND"


And I know you, Robert Bly,
drum-beater, chest-clutcher,
you probably made a sandwich immediately after.
Stroked a tasty kind of foreign mustard
onto bakery-fresh bread. I can see you holding it
in that hand,
you eat it all,
wipe your mouth,
all the while thinking about otters
or the Book of Ezekiel. You
wander your hallways, touching
everything that is not water or soap, God
damn it, Bly, for all I know
you went to bed, palm
against stubble, for all I know
you still
haven't listened
to what your mother
insisted when you were little,
after the window's sudden smack,
where you ran outside,
she, opening the window,
shrieking.

## NOTE TO THE GIRL IN THE BACK ROW
## OF THE POETRY READING


I did write a poem about you.
Like most of my poems, though,

something went awkward. No,
I didn't mention cows.

I talked about Hawaiian shirts.
And taking showers.

Okay, the reading was in a Borders
over where they sold bad coffee priced like something real.

In hindsight,
I should have bought an Ansel Adams coffee table book, marked
        30 percent off,

and offered it to you.
Instead, I read a few poems.

Every time I walked up to the stage, you watched me
like the flowing-haired model watches the Fabio on a romance title's
        cover.

When you stood up
and walked toward me,

I swear I wasn't about to mention pork rinds
or the human duodenum.

I wasn't going to say how "rhinotillexis" is the scientific name for
        nose picking.
I wasn't going to mention

that I secretly feared my pants smelled like fried chicken,
that it struck me so wrong when I saw "Now Accepting Credit Cards"
        hand-scrawled in red paint on the side of an ice cream truck,

so what
if the other guy reading that night writes poems

about guerilla warfare and hearts in ribcages, please don't sit down
        there,
the man is a rhinotillexomaniac,

I can tell you
all about it.

## I WANT TO HEAR SOME POEMS

that make me understand
where babies really come from,
why black holes happen,
why thunder makes me think of the color orange,

I want to know that I got out of bed this morning
for a reason,
I want to see two words rhyme
who never thought of each other that way before,

I want to hear political poems
that'd make Jefferson and Lincoln say, "Damn,
why didn't I think of that?"
words organized like the feathers on a peacock—
not like the frozen chicken spray painted blue
that says, "Good concept,
lousy follow-through."

I'm okay with a poem that's maybe more like a still life
as long as I can still taste the pomegranates in it
even if I've never tasted pomegranates before.

I don't want poems that lift me up where I belong
like an eighties ballad aching to rhyme "eagles fly" with "mountain
          high,"
I want poems to lift me
higher than where I belong
so I can look out and see what
could be, I want you to take a leap,
try a dactyl, a trochee, a simile, try iambic fucking goddameter

I want to hear poems that walk ahead of me
through the poison oak and thorn brushes, making paths for me
to follow;

and understand, I'm not asking a poem to save my soul, but
sometimes I want poems to remind me I've got something
worth saving and maybe point me
a way to start;

I don't just want poems to sing the word "love,"
I want poems that I can't help but fall for
because I want to fall in love
with you,
with me,
with someone I never expected,
so read me your poems,
I don't mean pull up your shirt and show me your cuts,
I mean let me feel the scars on my own skin;
don't tell me what to feel,
just break
my ice-choked heart.

I want your punch lines tiptoeing like ninjas
so I feel the joke before I have a chance to see it,

read me the difference between good and evil
as if you
were the explorer
who first came across that border,
hair standing up straight in the electricity of the disparity:

give me poems
that sway like fruit
on the centerpiece tree in the Garden of Eden
because I want you
to tempt me
with good,
with evil,
read me poems
that come in sparks off your tongue,
that I'll burn
to take with me
when you're done.

# TRACK 7

## WHEN YOU ARE ABOUT TO DIE

when you are three seconds from cracking the cracked concrete,
at the instant
the exit wound blooms across your jacket's back,
when the virus snaps you to screams over the thirty-six ninety-nine
            hotel room toilet, when the last drop of blood
sees your left ventricle, atrium, aorta
for the last time:

do you hope you will see Rick Astley?

You were in high school,
the headlines you didn't read were dripping
thrilling new diseases, cancers, heart attacks,
auto accidents, robberies gone wrong, badger attacks,
ill-conceived wars in Central America's boondocks,
and Rick Astley started singing,

*Never gonna give you up,*
*Never gonna let you down,*
*Never gonna run around and desert you.* His voice
soulful, powerful, a force of nature,
a voice both women
and men had to admit they burned to rub up against

because, Jesus, this was a voice to fix your car
and your dinner, write you a poem
and sell you a gun, goddamn
it was manly and it was
never gonna make you cry,
never gonna say goodbye,
never gonna tell a lie and hurt you.

And there you were, too young, largely,
for the fatal diseases, too young to become a Navy Seal,
watching Friday Night Videos as your parents slept upstairs,
and so what if you weren't out risking decapitation yet

in cars driven too fast on wet back roads with drunk friends,
because, after that obligatory Duran Duran,
you finally get to see what he looks like

and he appears
in the body of a gawky redhead.
Looks younger
than you. Can
not dance. Looks
in danger of being knocked over
by the model swaying next to him, Oh,
Death,

Oh, Death!

as my nose rockets toward the street,
as the daisies of my nerve cells drop each crackling petal,
as my brain spacewalks in the skull,
heartbeat stutters, bullet
hits the bone:

I have always visualized you
as brutal, with each fingernail meatier than my forearm,
no one
to be taken lightly,
no one to be taken
at all;

I pray, Oh, Death, three, two, one impact imminent,
hands slapping at my chest,
badger opening my ileum like a gum wrapper:

I pray
you can't dance
and look awkward
in the trench coat
draped over your shoulders.

# SIDE 2

# TRACK 1

## WHY INSTEAD OF BEGGING MY MOM FOR EXTRA ALLOWANCE MONEY SO I COULD BUY A RECORD ALBUM I SHOULD HAVE DECLARED VENDETTA ON THE ELECTRIC LIGHT ORCHESTRA

I was in love with a girl.
And I can say this with absolute certainty,
as I was in eighth grade,
and eighth graders know what love is

in ways that you all grow out of
with your big feet, bad skin, left at the pizza place and walking four
        miles so you don't have to call someone for a ride and
        explain,
your first kisses, shocking tongue in your mouth, cheeks turned
        floodplain "experience."

I didn't need experience.
I had Saturday afternoon movies on channel 6,
I had heart-in-fist dedications on Casey Kasem,
I had first-run *Love Boat* still on TV,

so fuck your coward jaded blissful first-hand knees-quaking "love,"
I was in love with a girl

and she wouldn't call me back.
I had tried everything.

And by "everything," I mean
every thing: I tried funny,
awkward,
self-deprecating,
I tried uncoordinated, I tried brainy,
I tried stories in class about Santa being hit by an airplane *Night
        Before Christmas* style (and
on the nose of the plane arose such a clatter, the pilot knew at once
        Saint Nick was a splatter)
everything.

I
was in love
with a girl,
and the months were winding that love so tight
it could slip and fly across the classroom and
crack
against the blackboard, I

was in love with a girl
and finally at the point,
sitting on the lion-print sheets of my bed,
of admitting love
was not enough—

     that love!
     was not!
     enough!

—to bend this universe as it needed to be bent.
I was in love with a girl
and sighed
and turned on my radio
to WOW or Sweet 98 or whatever the hell it was
and they said, *Here
is a new song
by ELO*,

and there's Jeff Lynne telling me "Hold on tight
to your dreams,"
even adding emphasis by rephrasing it in French, *Accroche-toi à ton
        rêve*,
and, damn, Universe,
you had me going,
I almost gave up on love—
on love!

In the hindsight of adulthood,

of thirty years unlearning what I learned that day,

of good dates, bad dates, eyelashes, bra straps,
yelling, *What the fuck do you want from me!* loud enough to be
       heard four apartments down,
heart-shaped cards, roses and rings, fourteen small teddy bears (one
       for every month),
poetry that said way too much about the goddamn moon,
the disproportionate surprise of warm breath on the inner ear,
that the Electric
Light
Orchestra

maybe could have been a little more specific.
That *Accroches-toi à ton rêve*, I never did look that up,
it might only mean: *Don't eat croutons*;

DJs are not waiting like archangels
to set the cosmos off their turntable wobble; they
tie up the request line talking to their girls,
making promises
that sound too much
like pop songs,

they're underpaid dudes
who put needles onto grooves
and let it
all
spin.

## DON'T STOP BELIEVING

*for Blair*


Over thirty years, this song has gone from awesome to meh,
just made it back to rock star awesome where you can now be
in your car, Steve Perry howling, *Hiding*
*somewhere*
*in the niiiiiiight!*
without feeling like a moron.

Some other song ends,
piano bum bum bum builds
to small-town girl, midnight train going anywhere. No:
goin' a-
ny-
where.

Mostly, it's the city boy.
Born and raised in south Detroit.
You made the song
yours with a poem you blended with it,
so it reminds me
as if the DJ just did that needleoffthevinyl scaree-eek
and broke in with a, *He*
*is gone, man.*
*Gone.*

I'm glad the song is cool again.
I'm glad I'm not crying to "Abacab" or "Private Eyes."
I still don't know what they mean by "streetlight people," but this
        works.

When you blew the auditorium open,
your operatic opening lifted thousands off their seats,
purple-crayoned beauty scrawling clouds into a clear night sky.
Your poems stay with me, ones
about payin' anything to roll the dice
just one more time,

the movie that never ends
but goes on
and on
and on
and on.

## FLOCK OF SEAGULLS

And it's not that A Flock of Seagulls means or meant much to you,
rising in the early days of music video with synthesizers so explosive
at a time *Rolling Stone* was asking if the guitar was finally dead;

this was 1982, man, and it was the fucking future,
all orange and pink spotlights and hair which defied physical laws;
more than their string of hit, their *and I ran, I ran so far away*,

was the wingspan, eagle, spaceship, seagull hair, see,
they were some European rock group with their album cover
wrapped around a slab of history

like some bigger-than-life president or event taking all the magazine
        covers hostage:
it's not the winter of '86, it's the winter of the Challenger disaster; not
        May of '77,
it's the May of *Star Wars*; not the summer of '82, it's Flock of fucking
        Seagulls.

So it's not you that's shaken, it's an epoch, an era, an arrow on your
        history book timeline
when a TV show looks back on them
and there's this happy, chubby guy with a baseball cap, somewhere in
        Florida and

this guy, nice guy,
had to've been working at a hardware store twenty years ago,
not wearing a spotlight like a boa;

it's like Reagan's still alive and working as a spokesman for a car
        dealership,
like the Tank Guy from the Tienanmen Square photo went on to make
        infomercials for an herbal colon-cleansing pill.
Maybe no one is who we thought they were,

or maybe they were
or kinda were or
were and weren't or

maybe it's us, not them, expectations
too heavy to carry through the rotations of decades,
of vinyl to cassette to CD to streaming,

where you ran,
you ran so far away
but, well,

you know the rest.

# TRACK 2

## THE LOST PARKING GARAGE OF TSOJCANTH

### Level 1

Just that morning, you couldn't remember his name;
running through a parking garage,
late to a meeting, and something
brought Dungeons & Dragons to mind;
maybe the grey,
maybe car stalls forming the kind of map squares
you spend hours tracing so nobody gets lost
and eaten by ogres or green slimes,
all of them forgetting their fireball spells and dropping the +2
        broadsword,
all that crap it took dice roll
after dice roll (after dice roll) to hoard
as we all sat in a dim-lit kitchen sharing dangers
real and invented, as all things in life and play are
in high school;
it all brought you
to him, the creator, the guy
with the perfect name for this, a name you knew
had sounds to it geeky and ferocious,
somehow bloodcurdlingly nerdy,
as you ran
to the meeting you were late for.

### Level 2

Back in the car, news on the radio
is two soldiers dead, the price of corn, more home foreclosures,
a man named Gary Gygax has died.

The announcer made an elf joke. Ha
ha. You sat and listened to the whole story, then drove
the dark maze
thinking of old friends, wild-looking dice,
legendary quantities of Mountain Dew.

Your eyes pursed
as you broke through the imaginary
door, into sunshine, these
familiar streets and trees
crowding in on you
like beasts.

# BECAUSE AARON RODGERS HAD A STACHE

which was not unlike the sunrise
in early September, 1540, which glowed awake on
what we now call the Grand Canyon
on that last full day before Spaniards with guns
laid words upon it,
starting the inevitable descent
to Flintstone-themed campgrounds, Bearizona Drive-Thru Wildlife
    Park, Burger Kings, that
final day belonging to the condors and bobcats,
pocket mice and bighorn sheep, all
who the Colorado River called to her banks.

Because Aaron Rodgers had a stache,
no "mustache," no, what he had was the highlight reel, even
as he stood with a bandaged shoulder under a sport coat,
nodding as another quarterback wore his shoes
and threw another interception, that was a stache
bobbing up and down encouragingly,
and it was more than any clean-shaven throw
off his back foot, hips wrenched the wrong way, 45-yard bullet
    straight to the playoffs
(scoff).

Because Aaron Rodgers had a stache
like molten chocolate
misted with cream
and the nonaddictive form
of a substance which would otherwise be
very, very illegal.

Because Aaron Rodgers had that stache
which was the sunrise
that day before Captain García López de Cárdenas
stepped to the south rim
under orders from the murderer Coronado to find the Seven Cities of
    Cibola,

a stache that deserved
to sit over Abe Lincoln's left shoulder on a mountain in South Dakota,
to be hewn from marble
and set on the National Mall between Jefferson and FDR,
be made monumental
by six brown Cadillacs at the entryway to Carhenge,
to be inscribed on the Statue of Liberty's open book,

no,
be lit in her hand,

because Aaron Rodgers had a stache
that my friends, sounding like conservationists fighting
for the survival of lions and Vikings and bears
(who all, incidentally, have some sort of mustache),
could be brought together to understand,

because Aaron Rodgers had the stache
that was honey and was milk,
that was steam engine and was Pong,
that was Macintosh, was peanut butter, was jelly,
and is, like this land from long ago,
no more.

## DISPROVING THE BON JOVI THEOREM

In his 1986 report, philosopher, mathematician, entertainer Jon Bon Jovi states, *I've seen a million faces and I've rocked them all.*

In the years since, our most skilled thinkers have lambasted Newton, scrutinized Einstein, spent countless hours trying to trisect an angle or solve Alhazen's billiard problem yet let Mr. Bon Jovi's claim stand untouched.

My esteemed colleagues: today I come before you to put Jon Bon Jovi to the test.

If we again look to the theorem as put forth in his work *Slippery When Wet*, we see that it has two parts to scrutinize.

The first, that he has seen a million faces, is one we do not need to spend time on. Records show how Mr. Jovi has sold over thirty-four million concert tickets, and even assuming many of these ticket sales are to concertgoers who follow him from show to show like some Jerry Garcia with more adorable hair, you can't deny that he has appeared before multiple millions and at least glimpsed some shades of their faces.

Stubborn skeptics might then contend, *Well, so he's seen over a million faces, he says he's only seen a million!* but the structure of Mr. Jovi's language is clearly meant to convey how he has seen not less than a million faces.

I state this confidently, my good colleagues, as I have two degrees in English and, as such, can claim the power, the knowledge, and the expertise of such accomplishment to assert that, barring some previously undisclosed malady of vision, Mr. Jovi has indeed seen a million faces.

But has he rocked them all? This is what we need to question, wondering, every concertgoer, every waitress, every masseuse, every heating and air conditioner repairman, every convenience store clerk, caddie, roadie, au pair, has he rocked every single face at least once?

We need to ask, as perhaps when Mr. Jovi was twelve and in the orthodontist's chair below Doctor Strangelove who, monthly, tightened Jonny's teeth and felt by no measure rocked by the young Bon Jovi's whimpers, *Eureka!* we might exclaim, *It is disproved!* But as Mr. Jovi only asserts how he has rocked them all but does not claim to have rocked each face every single time, we might also wonder if, fifteen years later, that tooth-tightener might not have sat in his BMW, top down, stopped at a red light, heard "Livin' on a Prayer" blaring from the Geo revving next to him, and felt his face at least somewhat rocked.

There lies the conundrum. There we must scour the world patiently, stopping each passerby, asking if they have knowingly had their face seen by Jon Bon Jovi and, if so, at any point in their life have they had that same face rocked under Mr. Jovi's influence?

You will find the questionnaire in the back of this book. Please fill it out truthfully and completely.

Your help is important as, despite having earned two whole degrees in English, despite the rights and privileges such honors hold, my resources are limited.

And, for the record, though I have only seen several thousand faces, I do feel that I have rocked nearly every one.

## YOU'RE IN YOUR FORTIES

*After "Do It to Me One More Time," "Escape (Piña Colada Song),"
and "Keep It Comin'"*


standing in a Food 4 Less,
looking at dandruff shampoos
or whatever, when you realize
the radio songs from when you were a kid were
all about penises.
It is suddenly
so out there,
the lyrics
about loving this or that way,
about don't stop it now, don't stop it, no, don't stop it now, don't
        stop:
penises.

And you feel dumb,
you never thought of it
like this cuz
you'd allow the contention that, sure,
you look on those days
as an innocence,
the world around you benign and sanitized,
sure, Pat Benatar mixed up your insides in an as-of-then indescribable
        way, sure,
you would concede the point that you knew nothing,
nothing, didn't
have the slightest idea,

still,

all the songs,
especially the corny ones,
because Devil Music like Blue Oyster Cult
really was asking for time to play B-sides

when they said, *Time to play B-sides,* whereas
Captain & Tennille, Rupert Holmes, KC & the Sunshine Band:
penis, penis, penis.

You end up
with Frosted Flakes and orange juice in your basket,
you roll out, sit in your car a few minutes,
thumbing down the dial,
looking for somewhere familiar
in this landscape so changed
from anything you recall.

## DANCING ON THE CEILING

Were they to try and break my hands off of you,
these would be no terra cotta hands, no
hands of porcelain or plaster, these hands
would hold you like the coconut husk
and—

no,
not the brown shell with the hair, I mean that green helmet thing
          around it that's not photogenic like the bit inside it
but,

okay,

were they to try and break my hands off of you, they would need
          rocks and machetes,
see,
because that outer coconut husk is a tough nut to shuck.

No foolin'.

I mean, see, these hands, these,

see, like, you are
the sun, you are
the rain—

damn it,

that's a Lionel Richie lyric.
Okay,
coconut.

Or not.

Let's start over,

my hands, my fingers really;
no no no no, my heart,

my heart's skyline
looks like rolling hills under a yawning dusky bruise of sky,

my heart crashes
big as oceans, my heart kicks
like a baby inside me
when you come near.

Top that, Lionel.
Once, twice, three times a lady,
boasting about all night long, you can have your husk,
your misshapen, green, stringy, husky heart, Lionel Richie,

coconut metaphors notwithstanding,
I love
like a redbud blossom
and you
just try
taking that
from me.

## ODE TO THE MORNING

When you
walk out of the bedroom, hair
styled eighties rock
by a pillow somehow,
turned Heart,
turned the high note of "How Do I Get You Alone"
except for the blur
still in your eyes,

you have green sweatpants
and nothing else on
as you stumble to the laundry room
for a bra or a shirt;

it's a vision

that turns the cords of nerves strung in my chest
to Christmas lights,
to colors blinking bright
as you
pass
by.

## GRADUATION ADDRESS TO THE KINDER KINGDOM AWESOME TOTS PRESCHOOL CLASS OF 2023

Graduates.

That's quite a word.
Three syllables.
Nine letters.
And a different meaning
for every one of you seated on the floor today.

For you, it means the first step into your future
as a pilot, an astronaut; for you,
it's mile marker one on your lifelong dream
of being a doctor, a veterinarian, a medical herpetologist; you
think it's a dinosaur with spikey wings; you
haven't heard a word I've said because you've been thinking about
        bunnies.

For all of you, it is a great beginning,
so get ready,
there ain't no naps in kindergarten, kids,
buckle your car seats and raise your game so you don't get surprised
        by the Gingerbread Man card on the Candy Land board of life.

And it's an honor to be here and receive this honorary degree of a
        PhΛBCD—
the other poets
will be jealous.

Now, if you carry one thing away
from my talk here today,
let it be an understanding of how you are all, right now, equally
        wonderful and cute. This
is a superficial world, you little dimplemongers,
and we only have a dollhouse-sized window to feel that special;

soon enough, we all get funneled into niches
by standardized tests, gym classes, hormones, clumsy parenting, bad
      economic decisions,
and more and more, and
your adorable little LEGO Towers of Babel don't stand a chance and,
      hey,

then you find yourself
thinking *The Iliad* kicks some real rear, Shakespeare's Prince Hal
      transforming into Henry Five, and that hardback *Collected*
      *Works of Robert Frost* blow your freaking minds,
so you end up majoring in English,
then working at Little King, making sandwiches,
then getting a master's degree in English,
then working at Little King, making sandwiches, and,

goddamn, you used to take Mensa tests for fun
and own them, but nobody gives a shit if you can explain the
      difference between William Wordsworth and William Carlos
      Williams,
and it gets cold
in January,
and you gotta keep the heat in your studio apartment at sixty,
and you're there,
sitting inside in an outside chair with those crappy plastic strappy
      things because
that's what you
can afford,
trying to fill the emptiness one Cheez-It at a time
because, hey, kids, "Cheez-It Saves!"

Or, listen:

we ain't born into heroes or born into kings,
because birthing isn't what writes your careers;
it's okay to love Keats or Broadway or *The Intelligent Investor* by
      Benjamin Graham,

love God, love Mozart, love baseball, love band;
there are voices in our heads from in and from out,
but all of us got one voice that tells us,
well,

tells us something that ain't crap. So listen
until you hear that.

And take a math class.
Just to be safe.
And floss. Nobody ever regrets
having flossed enough.

# THINGS TO DO WITH A TITLE BELT

1
If I had a title belt
like that one
on the wrestling star, that one
on *Rocky*'s Apollo Creed, that one
on the rodeo winner, Scottish Games hero, poetry slam champion,
I'd wear it to my day job,
be that coffee grinder, English teacher, haberdasher,
Jesuit, Salvation Army bell-ringer, cubicle warrior, I would wear it
vacuuming my bathroom, cooking eggs, adjusting my necktie,
      reading *The New York Times*,
I'd wear it to the grocery,
I'd wear it to the gas station, to the insurance office, to the space
      shuttle launch
where they'd have to be extra careful when they buckle those webs of
      straps over me
cuz I'll have people fired
if my belt gets scratched.

2
I'd wear it on dates.
Not to be pretentious,
I won't talk about it.
Unless she asks.

3
And don't squirm, I wouldn't wear
just the belt,
ever.
You pass these things on to others
and you don't want to imagine me,
and I don't want to imagine you
with Tom Cruise sunglasses as the sole accessory while you twirl in
      disco coolness around a living room or hallway
or alleyway or boulevard or city park or National Historic Site,
waving your parts in the breezes.

4

I'd sleep in it,
talk to it, drink beer with it,
I'd show it a good time, I would;
we'd get ice cream, go see some baseball, some theater, it would
        know
joy, we'd be inseparable in our time together
because I know how days can change,
how one shift in weather
and your car's under a tree,
family converts to wild religions, country goes too hastily into wars,
economies collapse, moths eat your best jacket, nothing lasts
long enough
but what you
put in the legwork,
the armwork, the headwork, the hipwork
to make, for its time,
true.

# TRACK 5

## NATURAL HISTORY

You can argue with reality,
insist that this Walmart surrounding you
has no right to exist, that this

was a concert venue bowling alley sand court volleyball bar,
that your journey to adulthood
has Historic-fucking-Landmark markers

right under that rack of $15 Classic Capri pants
(with easy comfort stretch), under those
tiki torches, *People* magazines, bargain bin Magic Bullet blenders,
    and

you might have a point. There is no authority,
now, able to undismantle the stage
you stood on next to Tortelvis himself at a Dread Zeppelin concert,

no zoning board to retroactively reclaim
the kiss so awkward
and so firework

that people should lay flowers at its feet every year
(and the red, white, and blue plastic bouquets piled nearby
do not do it that justice).

But what can you do?
Some farmer probably had to let his tomato field and house
slip away for the Ranch Bowl you remember, mumbling

about the son born right over there, the spot
the phone hung where he took that call,
and before him,

the tribes who valued this high ground,
the buffalo, mammoths, velociraptors,
the sea shells coiled into rock here hissing

about that mother fucking tortoise
who kept nipping at its cephalopod.
Motherfucker.

## HEARING THAT SONG AFTER TEN YEARS

It's astounding
what we let ourselves lose;
that music,
like a warm kiss on your ear,
like shivers that strum down your neck;
how do you forget,
how does some experience
leave your body
like the sunlight drips dark to the horizon,
like the neon buzzes lines across the window,
like the glass
sweats cold in your hand
as you mumble,
*forgive me,*
*forgive*
*me,*
as you forget
who you pray to
tonight.

## TOTAL ECLIPSE

What you don't suspect,
though you've known me
for years, is that I
    am in mid-interpretive dance,
        internally,
because we are on the interstate
headed to buy bread or to a movie or pick up a child,
restless on the radio, tuning
away from muffler commercials
or Bryan Adams songs, and you wonder
why I'm not changing
away from
this song,
you don't suspect
    my hands, you cannot see
    how they, acrobatically,
        roll a ball, stretch skyward,
            the gymnast in my soul
        bends back, then crouches, then leaps
    with such grace, oh,
1983, a year that is
to 1986 like Jim Steinman is to David Bowie
(you know, not as cool, not as lauded),
Bonnie Tyler's Welsh rasp
            (as I unroll the ribbon,
        one leg arcing upward),
I turned fifteen in 1983,
every now and then I fell apart,
I was not living in a powder keg
yet felt like I should have, as,
man, all fifteen-year-olds are giving off sparks,
we don't dare
let our faces show it,
we keep it
inside, don't let
the light

shine out, like,
like
something's blocking it or something, so
you don't suspect
           the opera,
                    the spectacle,
                             the fireworks
happening in the driver's seat next to you,
nothing I can say

as the radio plays
and the tires
scratch gravel
and whirr
and I just appear
to be watching
the road
as we drive.

# TRACK 6

## JOHN LENNON, YOKO ONO, AND YOUR MOM
## WALK INTO AN ELEVATOR


You're in Tokyo, wedding,
all your brothers and sisters;
back home, there are Beatles albums
all over. You're the youngest,
you mainly like Sgt. Pepper's for
the bright record cover big enough to wear
on your head like the Pope's hat. You refer to him
as John Lemon. The brother and sister
just above you, they ride the elevators,
hang out in the lobby, they plan, they are on a mission
to see this family
living in the penthouse.
It is 1977. Your dad
is doing incredibly for the time.
He was on the Big Island in 1941, he
saw planes fly low, signed up
in a breath. At home, he would complain
about Japanese cars as it still seemed possible
to think that everything
should be made in the USA.
He is here,
amazed by the lights,
the beauty of every smile.
The lesson you learn
is that there are no higher beings
on this earth, that all of us
stand just as human
when pressed close, that,
whether you're in line at the checkout
at a Brandeis store in Omaha
or in an elevator in the Hotel Okura,
it all sounds like home, *oh,*
*you have a lovely child, my sons and daughters*

*enjoy your music, how do you like Japan?* You
face the numbers
as they count 2, 3, 4, 5, 6, 7,
you don't turn around to stare
as you all rise together.

# TRACK 7

## ORIGIN STORY

I want a poem
like a gamma ray blast
when I've wandered out
on a New Mexico meadow,
beautiful, deserted,
never mind the razor wire and signs,
I want a poem
that'll fry me up green,
turn purple slacks to pom pom,
that takes an emotional peak
and cranks the dial to infinity;
ah,
sublime,
you wouldn't like me
when I'm sublime.

## LINES COMPOSED ON SEEING THERE IS
## AN AUTOGRAPHED COPY OF MY BOOK
## ON SALE FOR $7.99 AT HALF PRICE BOOKS


What happened, Daniel?
Was it something I said?
Or didn't say?
Was it just time?
Are you okay?
Did you move?
Was it a gift?
Not enough rhyme?
All of this?


People talk, Daniel;
my friend Bianca saw it
and sent a report right away,
poets, you know,
are the "unacknowledged legislators
of the world,"*                                              *Percy Bysshe Shelley
there is a network, Daniel,
you can't just dispose
of a book of poems
like this, Daniel,
without us knowing, Daniel,
sending memos
through the proper channels, negotiating
what needs to be done.


I get it, Daniel,
I have autographed copies
that needed to go, life
has its circumstances,
but
not like this, Daniel, not
like this:
I fed a book of Gary Snyder's
to a deer, set a copy

of Marjorie Saiser's
onto a gravel road in rural Nebraska,
made a drum from Robert Bly,
buried Pattiann Rogers
in the garden
with a row of possum teeth,             .
there
are ways
to do this,
Daniel,
there is
a code
which you
have not
seen fit
to heed.
So we,
your unacknowledged overlords,
are scribbling charters, briefs, manifestos, and warrants
to determine
our course of action on
your
misdeed.

## AT THE PARK WITH MY DAUGHTER

The dinosaur grins.
And it's not a real dinosaur.

I point this out
so you don't worry
about our safety.
Or if this is a real poem.

Ask around.
Most of the poets you know
will back me up.

Except Todd.

Fuck you, Todd.

It's tough to tell
if it's a Tyrannosaurus
or a Velociraptor,

could be an Allosaurus,
but nobody talks about Allosauruses these days.

They're not trendy.
So nobody makes playground bouncy shapes
that look like an Allosaurus.

Anyway, it's green.
My daughter used to love
sitting on its saddle
and springing pell-mell around.

Sorry,

I'm still caught up
in the whole Todd thing.

Why don't you think it's a poem, Todd?
You can do better?
Don't want dinosaurs in your poems, Todd?
The f-word too blunt for your toolbox,
motherfucker? "Motherfucker" too motherfucker
for your motherfucker, motherfucker?

Motherfucker.

Stop hanging out with Todd.
Go to a park instead.
I know a good one.
It has a dinosaur.
There's this amazing poem about it.

## SO MUCH DEPENDS

*so much depends*
*upon*

*a red wheel*
*barrow*

*glazed with rain*
*water*

**beside the white**
**chickens**

is why I hated poetry.
It was in every textbook
every year of high school. Every year
we read it

and failed to achieve a greater understanding
of chickens,
wheelbarrows,
existence.
This is why, I think, teachers
have a hard time teaching poetry.
They assign this
and then have to ask questions

like, *What do you think it means?*
*What is it that depends upon this?*
They may do this
not out of a lesson plan
but from their own curiosity,
hoping one of us will say something
which makes sense.

There's a nice story behind why the poem was written.
The story works better than the poem for me.

It's the kind of poem
you may be forced to write an essay on
where you analyze the meter
and the word choice
and reveal why
it is sometimes called the masterwork
of American 20th-century poet William Carlos Williams.

I think you should read "The Widow's Lament in Springtime"
instead.

William Carlos Williams has taught me
more about where to break
lines than any other poet;
William Carlos Williams,
I came to discover,
I like.

Not in high school.
Not with glazed chickens,
wet wheelbarrows,
red,
and white,
and depending.

## DEAR POET

*I have left no immortal work behind me—nothing to
make my friends proud of my memory—but I have
lov'd the principle of beauty in all things, and if I had
had time I would have made myself remember'd.*
—John Keats, February 1820 letter to Fanny Brawne


Dear Poet
who did not waste time
in the chains of his own dramatics
as too many of us have done,
whose preoccupations with death were brought about
by the blood more in his throat
than in his heart, the mortality
of his own white cheeks:

You were not drunk, you were not spinning
idiocy into adventurous exaggeration, you

just living in whichever garden
would open a gate to you, whatever journal
that would deign to be blackened by your words:
light our ways, good sir, stay close;
help us all to recognize the beauty you treasured,
that we, as you, might be so unremembered.

# APPENDIX A

Questionnaire:

1. Has Jon Bon Jovi ever seen your face?
☐ Yes (Go to Question 2)
☐ No (Skip Question 2)

2. Has he rocked it?
☐ Yes
☐ No

Please return surveys to:
    Bon Jovi Survey
    9712 N 34th St
    Omaha, NE 68112

# ACKNOWLEDGEMENTS

I owe thanks to the following periodicals and anthologies, in whose pages these poems first appeared:

*Cave Wall*: "The Lost Parking Garage of Tsojcanth"
*Drunk in a Midnight Choir*: "Natural History"
*FreezeRay Poetry*: "Total Eclipse"
*Green Mountains Review*: "On Kansas 156"
*Ibbetson Street*: "Origin Story"
*In the Company of Rogues: Poets of the Rogues Gallery*: "I Wish"
*Oakwood*: "It is 1997, karaoke bar, Des Moines"
*Pilgrimage*: "When You Are About to Die"
*Plains Song Review*: "John Keats," "Shelley"
*Rattle*: "Why Instead of Begging My Mom for Extra Allowance Money So I Could Buy a Record Album I Should Have Declared Vendetta on the Electric Light Orchestra"
*Time Flies/Time Stands Still*: "Rapture"
*Tipton Poetry Journal*: "Note to the Girl in the Back Row of the Poetry Reading," "Ted Kooser"

# ABOUT THE AUTHOR

Matt Mason is the Nebraska State Poet and was Executive Director of the Nebraska Writers Collective from 2009–2022. Through the US State Department, he has run workshops in Botswana, Romania, Nepal, and Belarus. Mason is the recipient of a Pushcart Prize, and fellowships from the Academy of American Poets and the Nebraska Arts Council. His work can be found in *The New York Times,* on NPR's *Morning Edition,* in *American Life in Poetry,* and more. Mason's 4th book, *At the Corner of Fantasy and Main: Disneyland, Midlife and Churros,* was released by The Old Mill Press in 2022. Matt is based out of Omaha with his wife, the poet Sarah McKinstry-Brown, and daughters, Sophia and Lucia.

# BOOK RECOMMENDATIONS FROM THE AUTHOR

*peluda* by Melissa Lozada-Oliva

Melissa Lozada-Oliva's *peluda* is what a book of poetry should be. She takes perfectly-crafted lines and reimagines what a poem can be and do with poems structured wonderfully, both in how they look on the page and in the sounds she weaves them together with. These are poems that make you laugh and, when your guard is down, punch you in the stomach with lines like: "if you ask me if i am fluent in Spanish i will tell you my Spanish is an itchy phantom / limb—reaching for words & only finding air" (from "Ode to Brown Girls With Bangs").

*Still Can't Do My Daughter's Hair* by William Evans

William Evans' *Still Can't Do My Daughter's Hair* is a book of poems on parenthood. Which means it's a book about something else: "parenthood" means a person is responsible for the life of another while and also reliving their own past experiences through them, marveling at what's similar and what is unfathomable. In these poems, Evans writes about his own father, his wife, his daughter, and the world in which he's seen death in the news and in person. And these poems come out beautifully, with lines like these from the title poem: "I fear her scalp/ will know I'm a fraud" or describing his father as ". . . a wind chime so heavy it doesn't even make a sound." This is an incredible book that at times can seem hard to read but far harder to put down.

*Afterwards* by Reagan Myers

Reagan Myers' *Afterwards* hit me like a textbook for choosing the right details so that a poem feels like your own experience, not like the experience of someone else. Lines like: ". . . not me/who used the unpaid bills as coasters./She is the broken spot on my shower head,/she drips and drips, fills my ears" bring these poems clearly into a reader. The book meditates on death, with poems about friends, family, artists who have died but also poems about how our own culture, even our own selves urge us on toward death through abuse and depression. Through it, Myers beautifully makes these poems more than about grief, with humor (Mayor Duke, the dog elected mayor of a town in Minnesota) and hope.

## OTHER BOOKS BY BUTTON POETRY

If you enjoyed this book, please consider checking out some of our others, below. Readers like you allow us to keep broadcasting and publishing. Thank you!

Desireé Dallagiacomo, *SINK*
Dave Harris, *Patricide*
Michael Lee, *The Only Worlds We Know*
Raych Jackson, *Even the Saints Audition*
Brenna Twohy, *Swallowtail*
Porsha Olayiwola, *i shimmer sometimes, too*
Jared Singer, *Forgive Yourself These Tiny Acts of Self-Destruction*
Adam Falkner, *The Willies*
George Abraham, *Birthright*
Omar Holmon, *We Were All Someone Else Yesterday*
Rachel Wiley, *Fat Girl Finishing School*
Bianca Phipps, *crown noble*
Natasha T. Miller, *Butcher*
Kevin Kantor, *Please Come Off-Book*
Ollie Schminkey, *Dead Dad Jokes*
Reagan Myers, *Afterwards*
L.E. Bowman, *What I Learned From the Trees*
Patrick Roche, *A Socially Acceptable Breakdown*
Rachel Wiley, *Revenge Body*
Ebony Stewart, *BloodFresh*
Ebony Stewart, *Home.Girl.Hood.*
Kyle Tran Mhyre, *Not A Lot of Reasons to Sing, but Enough*
Steven Willis, *A Peculiar People*
Topaz Winters, *So, Stranger*
Darius Simpson, *Never Catch Me*
Blythe Baird, *Sweet, Young, & Worried*
Siaara Freeman, *Urbanshee*
Robert Wood Lynn, *How to Maintain Eye Contact*
Junious 'Jay' Ward, *Composition*
Usman Hameedi, *Staying Right Here*
Sean Patrick Mulroy, *Hated for the Gods*
Sierra DeMulder, *Ephemera*
Taylor Mali, *Poetry By Chance*
Matt Coonan, *Toy Gun*

Available at buttonpoetry.com/shop and more!

## BUTTON POETRY BEST SELLERS

Neil Hilborn, *Our Numbered Days*
Hanif Abdurraqib, *The Crown Ain't Worth Much*
Sabrina Benaim, *Depression & Other Magic Tricks*
Rudy Francisco, *Helium*
Rachel Wiley, *Nothing Is Okay*
Neil Hilborn, *The Future*
Phil Kaye, *Date & Time*
Andrea Gibson, *Lord of the Butterflies*
Blythe Baird, *If My Body Could Speak*
Andrea Gibson, *You Better Be Lightning*

Available at buttonpoetry.com/shop and more!